Starting Points edited by Henr

Let's ...
Patte...

Rita Davies

Evans

Evans Brothers Limited London

Read this first

Pattern, shape and design are all important in our daily life. Some are natural patterns like a honeycomb and others are man-made like a block of flats.

Abstract drawings are often simply taking one kind of shape or pattern and exaggerating or repeating it in a model or a picture. Look at some pictures by artists like Picasso, Matisse or Mondrian and you will soon begin to see how to use colour, shape, line and texture when making patterns of your own.

Some of the suggestions in this book will give you a chance to experiment with your own ideas for book covers, wall hangings and place mats; or simply to enjoy using different materials such as paint, crayon and paper.

I hope the ideas in this book will be fun to try out and will encourage you to look at all the variety of shape and pattern surrounding you at home, at school and in the street.

A fantastic face pattern.

Fantastic patterns

Collect together
Crayons and chalks
Kitchen or sugar paper
Black or coloured ink

How to start

1. Draw the outline shape of a face, animal or fish to fill the whole of your paper.
2. Now divide your shape into areas or sections for colouring.
3. Colour your picture with crayon or chalk. Don't just make flat areas of colour but experiment with circular or zig-zag lines. Divide parts into small squares or triangles to be filled in with crayon or chalk. Make your picture as fantastic as you can.
4. Paint the background with a contrasting coloured ink or paint, Sweep your brush over your design for an unusual effect.

Draw a bold outline.

Brush ink or paint over the picture.

Now experiment
Look at pictures of odd faces or fantastic animals drawn by artists like Paul Klee.

Try limiting your colour scheme or repeating one shape, perhaps a fish, many times on your paper.

The ink brushed over the picture gives an interesting effect.

Growth patterns

Collect together
Oil pastels or crayons
Black or grey sugar paper

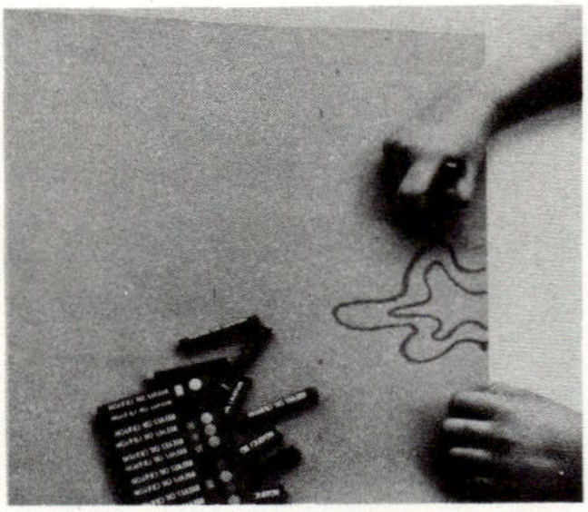

Start the growth pattern.

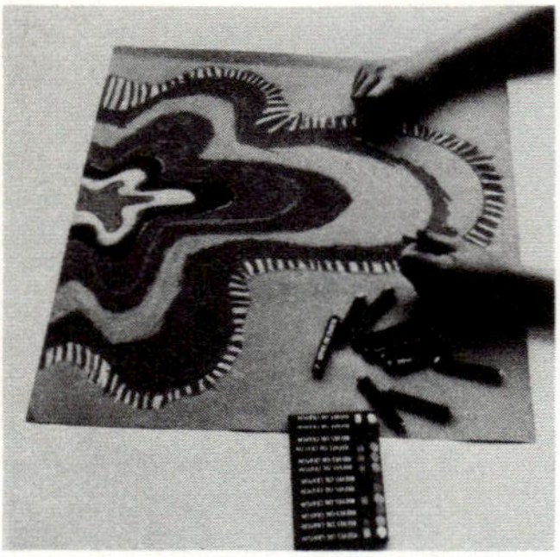

Fill in the spaces.

How to start

1. Make a small, many curved line 'grow' from the centre of one edge of the paper.
2. Repeat this again above the first line. Follow the curves but sometimes come in near to the original line and sometimes widen the gap.
3. Carry on building up the shape in lines so that it grows out irregularly in all directions across the paper.
4. Colour each section with flat areas of colour, zig-zag lines or circles.

Now experiment
Using black paper, limit yourself to only two or three bright colours.

Instead of curved lines try repeating a straight line shape. This time take care to repeat the original shape exactly as the pattern grows, leaving the same amount of space in between.

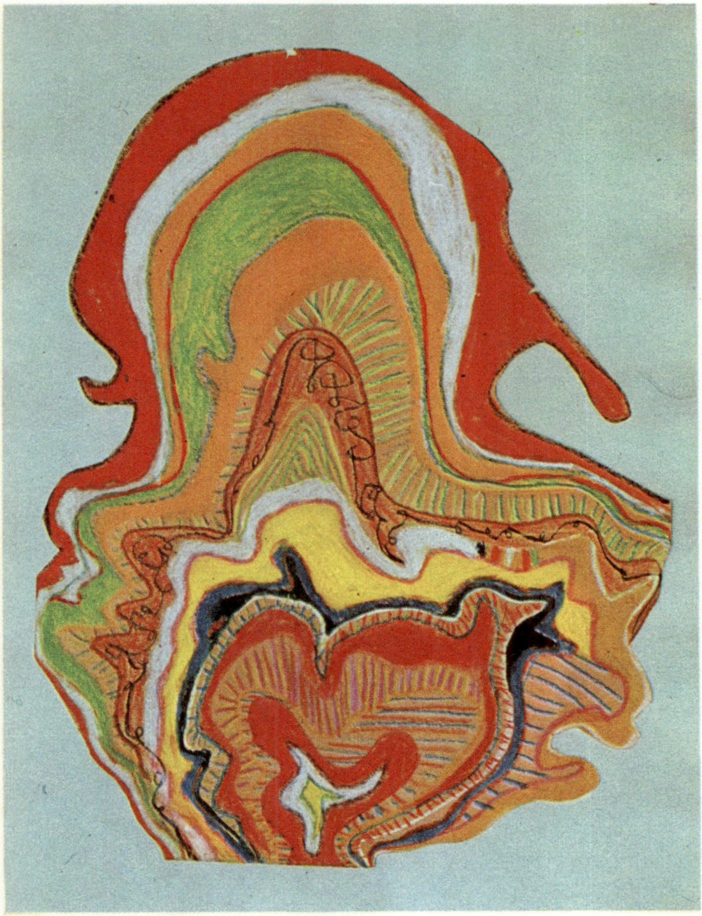

Many different ways have been used to colour this growth pattern.

Ink splatter patterns

Collect together
Two or three old toothbrushes
Waterproof ink or thinly mixed powder paint
Cartridge paper or card
A variety of objects and card shapes

How to start
1. Place a number of objects such as a pair of scissors, a comb, pencil, etc. on to a sheet of paper.
2. Dip a toothbrush into ink and shake the excess back into the bottle.
3. Hold the brush above the objects in one hand and move the first finger of your other hand across the bristles, spraying the ink on to the objects.
4. Keep moving the brush so that the ink does not spray on one place only.
5. Remove the objects to reveal their silhouette shapes beneath.

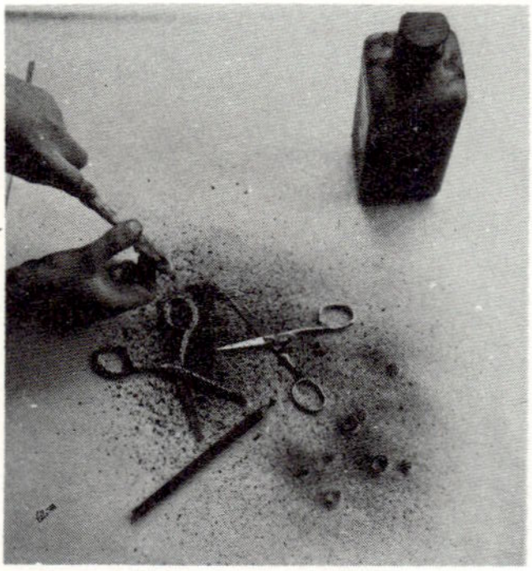

Spatter the ink.

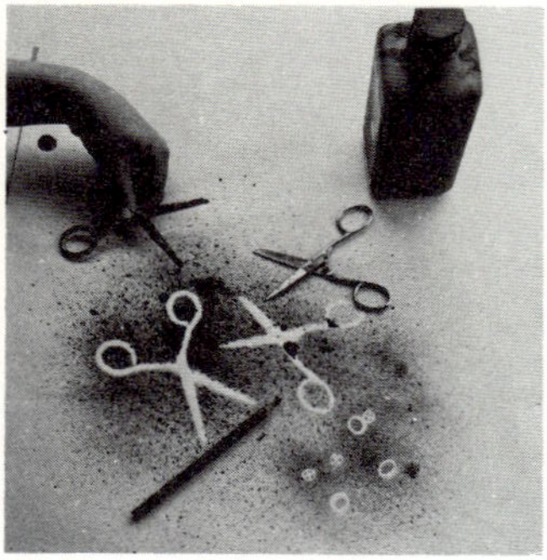

Remove the objects to see the pattern.

Now experiment
This technique needs a lot of experiment before it is really successful. Find out how much ink you need on the bristles and develop your own style for spraying ink evenly over the paper.

Cut some card shapes with interesting edges and make a pattern of them on a

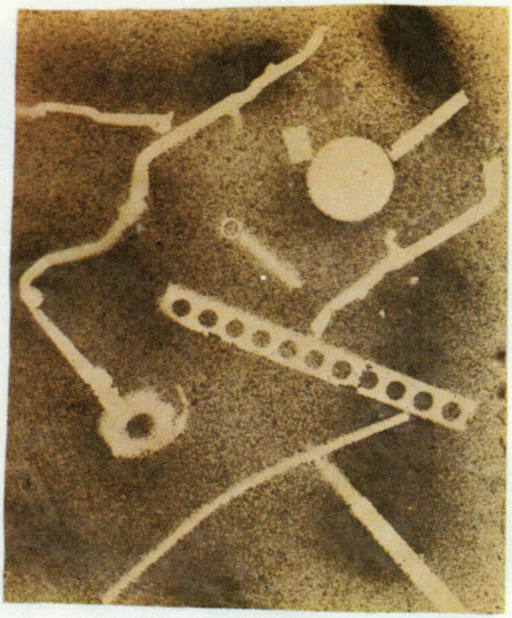

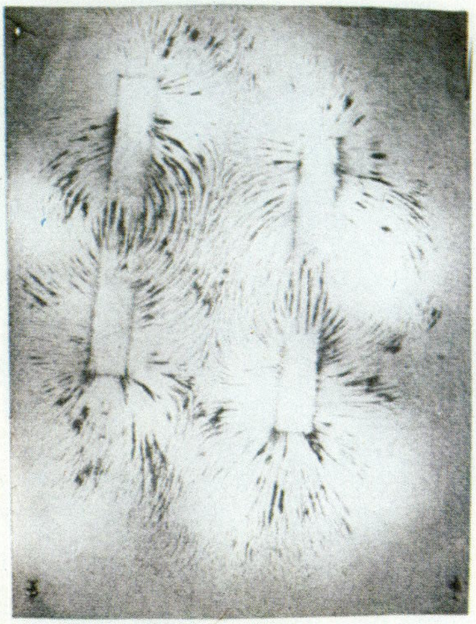

Two ink splatter patterns.

sheet of paper before spraying them with a variety of colours.

Try using a gold or silver aerosol spray as a change from paint or ink.

Remember that objects like scissors will now be permanently gold!

Cut-out shapes or plastic doileys can make interesting patterns and designs for cards.

Take a shape

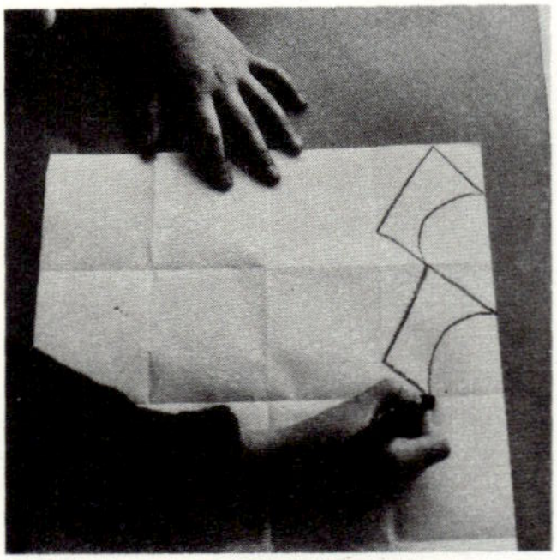
Repeat your shape in each section.

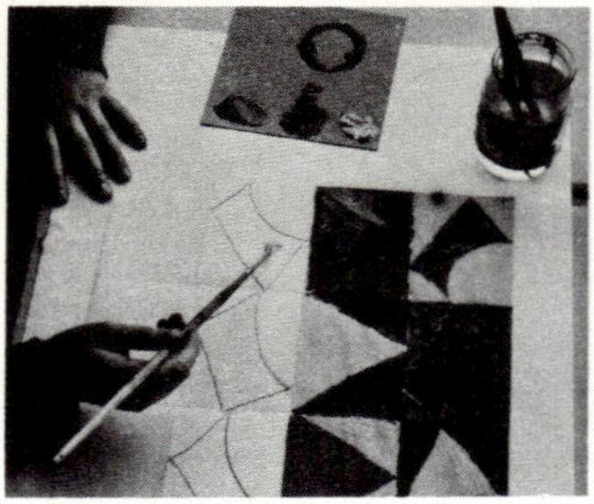
Paint the pattern.

Collect together
Paints or printing colours
Brushes
Jar of water
White kitchen paper

How to start
1. Fold a sheet of paper in half, then into quarters and eighths. (If the paper is large enough, fold it into sixteen sections.)
2. Practise on a rough sheet of paper until you have an interesting shape to fill one of the sections.
3. Repeat this shape in each of the sections.
4. Paint the sections, limiting yourself to three colours.
5. Alternate the colours so that if, for example, you are using red, yellow and blue; the first shape is red with a yellow background, the second yellow with a blue background, the third blue with a red background, and so on.

Now experiment
Make a pattern using two basic shapes, repeating them alternately on the sheet of paper.

Try using cut-out coloured paper shapes stuck into the sections.

This pattern has used two different shapes.

This technique may encourage you to experiment with designs for painting or printing on material. A water-based printing ink, such as the one made by Rowney, can be used and can be made permanent. A mixture of powder colour with liquid glue or detergent also works well.

Take a square

Collect together
A sheet of black paper
Several sheets of coloured paper
Glue
Scissors
Some sheets of white paper

How to start
There are several ideas you can experiment with.

1. Cut a square of black paper into pieces and re-arrange them on a coloured background.
2. How many different-sized squares can you cut from one large square. Arrange these in a regular and irregular pattern.
3. Can you cut a red paper square, 5 cm × 5 cm, into a series of rectangles and re-arrange them on a yellow square 10 cm × 10 cm?
4. Collect together all your different coloured squares and try various arrangements; some on top of each other, others with a corner or edge touching. Arrange them on a contrasting coloured background.

Now experiment
Try using circles, triangles and rectangles in the same way. Arrange

These squares are being arranged according to size.

Consider your arrangement carefully.

A dark background makes these squares stand out.

and combine them in a series of designs.

Remember that in all your experimenting it is important to look at the shapes in relation to each other. Never glue a single shape without seeing its place in the overall design.

Symmetrical patterns

This really follows on from the last idea but now you will need to organise your shapes so that they balance. This is called symmetry.

Collect together

Some sheets of black and white paper
Glue
Scissors

How to start

1. Cut a piece of white paper into a rectangle and then cut a piece of black paper exactly the same size.
2. Cut the black rectangle into three equal pieces.
3. Fold the black pieces in half vertically.
4. Cut along the edges of the folded paper making a simple, flowing line.
5. Open out the folded strips. Cut along the fold of one of them.
6. Arrange the pieces on the white rectangle using the two halves at each end. Try and make a balanced pattern.

Now experiment

Mount a coloured square on a larger sheet of paper. Cut into all four sides (but not the corners) pulling out the shapes. Do not throw any pieces away. Glue the pieces to the background paper.

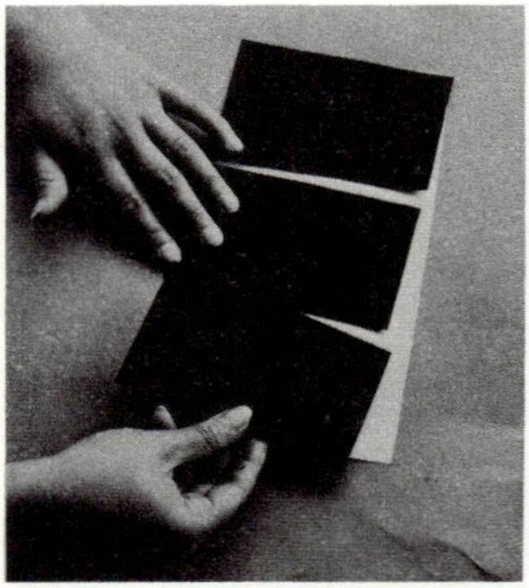

Take the three black pieces . . .

. . . fold them in half and cut along the edge . . .

. . . and arrange them on the white paper.

Two ways of cutting into a square and pulling out the pieces.

Try not to lose the original square shape with this method, even though pieces have been pulled out.

You could adapt this method using a triangle instead of a square.

Distorted shapes

Collect together
A sheet of black sugar paper
A smaller square of coloured paper
Black felt tip pen or crayon
Ruler Scissors

How to start
The aim is to make a straight line design become curved. It may sound difficult but it only needs care in cutting and arranging the pieces.

1. Draw a thick black strip from corner to corner across the square of coloured paper. Use the ruler to get the edges straight.
2. Now divide the square into 1 cm strips.
3. Cut out the strips and re-arrange them on the black paper so that the straight black line becomes curved. This means that you must move the strips slightly upwards or downwards as well as at an angle. At the same time make sure that the edges form a pleasing pattern. A simple fan-shaped arrangement is one way to do this, or a curved pattern including two fan shapes in the one design.

Make sure you are not near an open door or window. It won't be fun if all your strips of paper are blown away.

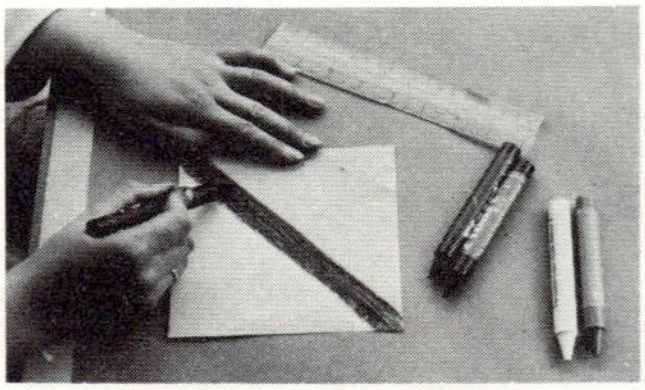

Colour the black strip.

Arrange the strips carefully.

You could add other bands of colour to your paper before cutting.

Now experiment

Find an interesting picture of people or animals. Cut it into equal strips and re-arrange them in straight lines with space in between. Concentrate on the spaces between the strips, making some narrow and some wide. If you have two copies of the same picture try cutting one from top to bottom and the other from side to side and compare the different results.

Experiment with different pictures of people and faces. Make thin people fat or give faces odd expressions.

Magazine collage patterns

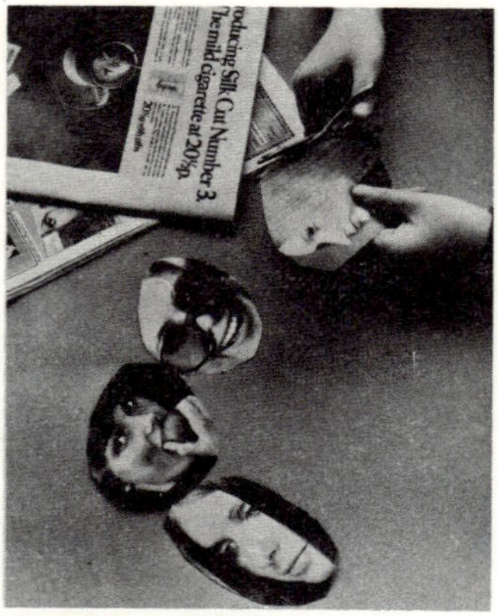

Cut out faces for a pattern.

Collect together
Some magazines
Scissors Glue
Sheets of background paper

How to start

1. Look through a number of magazines and cut out as many people—or parts of people—as you can.
2. Make a collage just using faces or arms. Arrange them closely together, sometimes overlapping, and glue them to the background paper.
3. If you are using faces you could group them together to show 'sadness', 'laughter' or 'anger'.

Now experiment
Try making up odd combinations. Put a baby's head on a lady's body with a pair of football boots to finish off! Make a series of peculiar people.

Make an abstract picture based on one colour scheme, for example all warm colours such as red, orange and yellow. Tear out pieces from magazines and glue them down, overlapping each other, so that no background shows.

Cut out different-sized letters or numbers and arrange them in a pattern.

A paper collage of faces.

Tissue paper patterns

Collect together
Sheets of coloured tissue paper
Scissors
PVA adhesive and brush
Sheets of background paper

How to start
1. Take three differently coloured sheets of tissue paper.
2. Cut these into long strips about 4 cm wide.
3. Arrange the strips, mixing the colours, lengthways on the paper and touching each other.
4. Thin the PVA adhesive with water so that it is like milk and brush it on to *both* sides of the strips before gluing them down.
4. Choose *one* of the colours already used and cut strips to fit, widthways, on the paper.
5. Arrange and glue these strips with gaps between them to reveal the colours underneath.
6. Brush adhesive across your design so that there will be a glossy look to your pattern when it is dry.

What effect does the overlapping tissue have on the other colours?

Stick the first layer of strips.

Add the second layer.

Choose the colours you use carefully.

Now experiment

You can use this 'tissue glazing' idea on top of your crayon, paint or paper patterns. Simply coat both sides of a sheet of tissue paper with the PVA adhesive and stick it over the design. This will not only give a shiny effect, but will also merge and blend the colours of the design according to the colour of the tissue paper.

Marbling

Collect together
Small bottles of oil-based inks such as Lin marbling inks
Vinegar
A bowl of water
Small sheets of cartridge paper
Newspaper

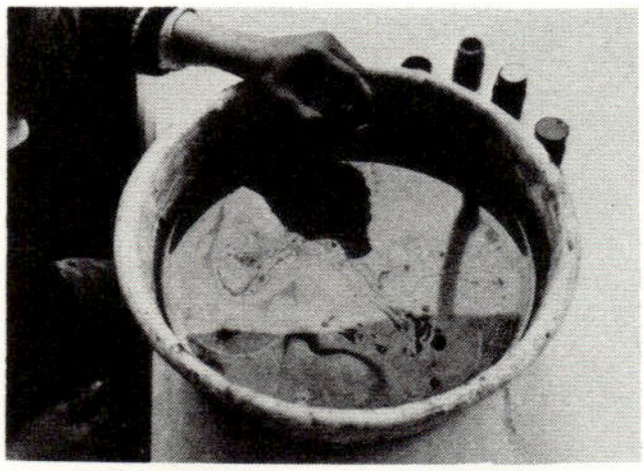

Drip the ink in slowly.

The paper has picked up the ink.

How to start
1. Cover a table with newspaper for your finished patterns.
2. Carefully drip some ink colours on to the water in the bowl.
3. Add a sprinkle of vinegar to help break up the oil colours.
4. Gently swirl your finger around in the water to move and merge the inks.
5. Holding two corners of a sheet of paper, pull it through the water so that it picks up the oily colours. You should get a twirling, marble effect and no two patterns will ever be the same.

Now experiment
Instead of pulling the paper through the water, cut a piece the size of the bowl and gently rest it on the top. Lift the paper carefully so that the ink pattern is on one side only.

If you cannot get any oil-based inks try this method using oil paints.

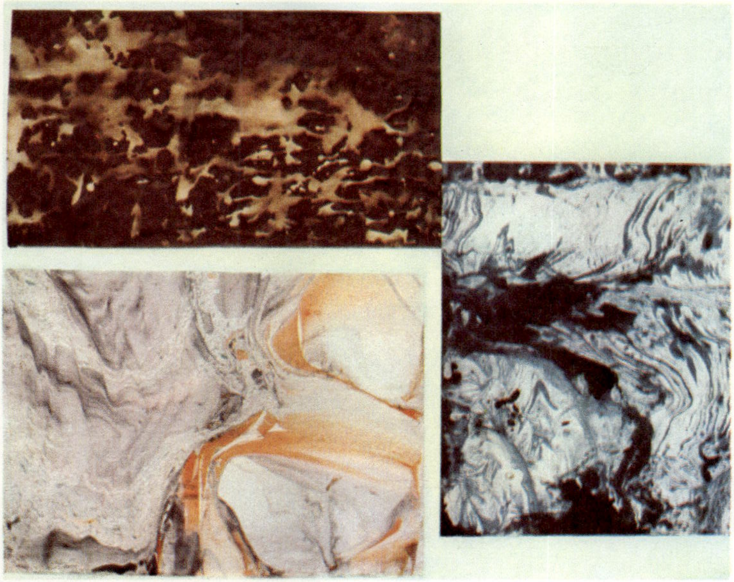

Some marbled patterns.

Sprinklings of powder paint also give an unusual result. You will not need vinegar for this method.

Seed patterns

Collect together
A variety of different kinds of seeds, dried peas, beans and lentils
PVA adhesive
Card
Spatula or brush

How to start
1. Work on a fairly small piece of card about 20 cm × 25 cm.
2. Divide the card into sections with curved or straight lines.
3. Fill in each section with seeds. Carefully coat a small area with glue and then press the seeds into it, one by one.
4. When you have finished your pattern, dilute some of the adhesive with water until it is like milk. Then cover the whole pattern. This will ensure that no seeds fall off and, when it is dry (in about a day), your pattern will have a shiny, transparent coat.

Now experiment
Paint a completed seed design, keeping the colours to the separate sections.

Make a face pattern with the seeds and paint the background so that it stands out.

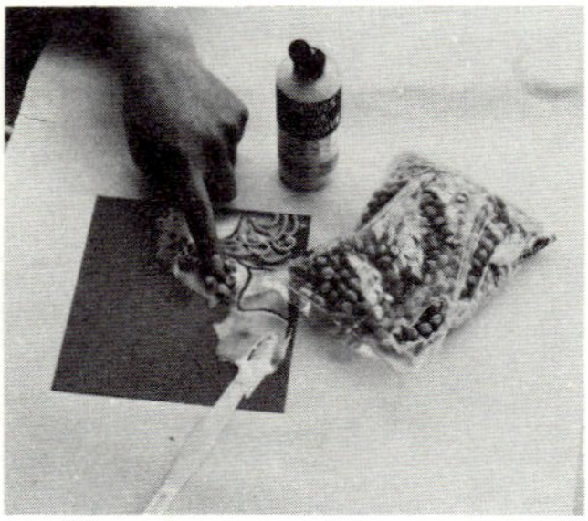

Only glue a small section at a time.

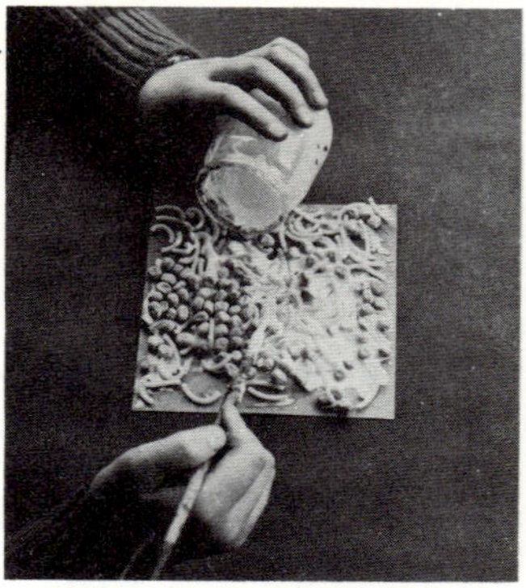

Cover your finished pattern with adhesive.

An unfinished seed pattern.

Pencil patterns

Collect together

Drawing pencils graded from HB to 4B
Sheet of cartridge paper

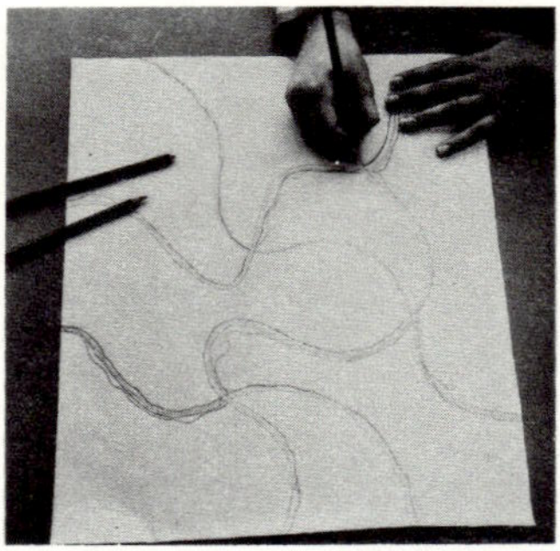

Follow the lines closely . . .

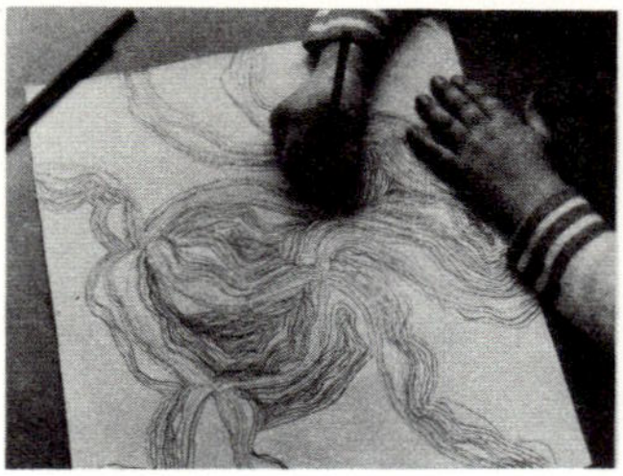

. . . to build up an interesting pattern.

How to start

1. Draw a curved, snaky line from one edge of the paper to the other.
2. Repeat this so that there are about five snaky lines going across the paper in different directions.
3. Now follow the curves of the lines repeating them very closely until the paper is filled with a wavy pencil pattern.
4. Use different kinds of black pencil leads to get a variety in the lines.

Now experiment

Try using coloured pencils instead of black lead ones.

Instead of curvy lines draw straight lines with angles and corners.

You could use wool or string to make the lines. Use a strong PVA adhesive spread over the card and press the wool into it while it is still wet.

This pattern was drawn with different coloured pencils.

Crayoned name patterns

Collect together
Wax crayons   Pencil
Sheet of white cartridge paper
Iron

How to start

1. Fold the cartridge paper in half lengthways so that there is a crease down the centre.
2. Work on one half of the paper only.
3. Write your name in double-lined capital letters with a pencil. Make sure that each letter touches the next and that they go from the top of the paper to the crease.
4. Colour your name thickly with wax crayons.
5. Fold the paper in half again and with a warm iron press the two halves together. You may need a grown-up to help you with this.
6. Open out the paper and you will find that your name has been transferred to the other half of the paper.
7. Colour both names and the background. Turn the paper round, so that the crease runs from top to bottom, and you will find a symmetrical pattern.

Fill in the letters with different colours.

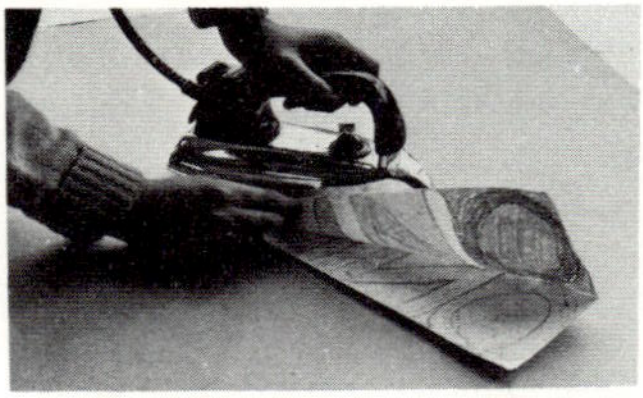
The iron will transfer the design.

Can you read the name?

Now experiment

Make these transfer patterns with other words as well.

Limit your colours to two or three so that the final result is a balanced pattern in colour as well as shape.

Lino printing

Lino cutting is quite difficult and has many stages. It is well worth persevering until you master each step. You will probably need someone to help you.

Keep your picture simple.

Collect together

Lino tools—these should include a selection of blades and a handle
Lino Tray
Paint roller and printing inks
Cartridge paper
Felt tip pen

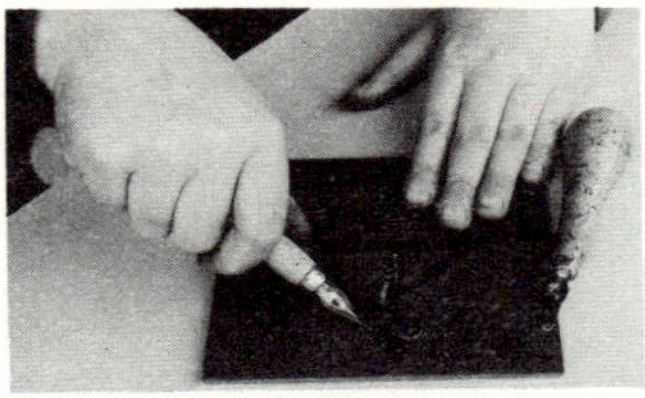

This is the correct position for your hands when cutting.

How to start

1. Begin with a bold and simple design. Draw the outline with a felt pen on to the lino.
2. Before you start to cut the lino make sure that you are holding the tool correctly as in the picture.
Both sets of fingers must be behind the cutting edge and all the cutting must be away from your body.

Roll out the ink in a tray.

3. Start cutting with a V-shaped cutter making an even groove along the edge of the design.
4. Squeeze some colour into a tray and roll it out. Now ink the lino block by rolling the colour on to it.

Ink the lino.

5. Place the lino, ink side down, on the top corner of the paper. Make sure

A series of lino prints.

you get a good print by pressing it down with a clean roller.

6. Repeat this print a number of times. Remember to ink the block after each print.

7. Wash the lino and the roller clean and then make further cuts in the lino to add to your design. Mark the back of the lino with an arrow to show the top.

8. Go back to stage 4 but this time use a different coloured printing ink. Place the block as carefully as possible over the first print and press it down with a clean roller.

9. When you remove the block you will see some of the original colour as well as an overprint of the second colour.

10. Clean the lino and roller again and then cut some more of the design away, this time, perhaps, cutting away the background. Print the block using a third colour.

Now experiment

There are so many different ways you can experiment with lino cuts and as you practise and get better you will be able to think of ideas of your own.

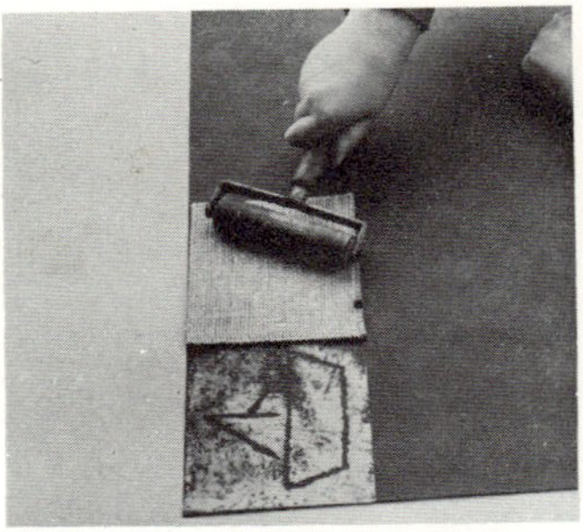

Press hard with the clean roller.

The first print.

The second print after further cutting.